Tiny Houses

A Complete Step-By-Step Guide to Designing, Building and Living In A Tiny House On A Budget

Dianne Selton

© **2016**

Dianne Selton Copyright © 2016

All rights reserved. No part of this publication may be reproduced, distributed, or transmitted in any form or by any means, including photocopying, recording, or other electronic or mechanical methods, without the prior written permission of the publisher, except in the case of brief quotations embodied in critical reviews and certain other noncommercial uses permitted by copyright law.

Although the author and publisher have made every effort to ensure that the information in this book was correct at press time, the author and publisher do not assume and hereby disclaim any liability to any party for any loss, damage, or disruption caused by errors or omissions, whether such errors or omissions result from negligence, accident, or any other cause.

Table of Contents

Introduction

Pros & Cons of Tiny House Living

Financing a Tiny House

The Houseboat

About Yurts

Tiny House RV

The Traditional Tiny House

Four Basic Floorplans

A Little About Gathering Your Materials, Tools, AC, Lighting

Building Your Kitchen, Bathroom

Tiny Home Tips, Buy vs Build

Conclusion

Introduction

The first thing that you need to know about Tiny Houses is what they truly are. They are an affordable and practical way to live in a home, and a move towards living more simply. Granted it can be frustrating to get started. In our minds we compare Tiny House living with living in a large home with its clutter and every modern luxury. Our standards may be high and we may fear "going without". But Tiny Homes are sustainable, sleekly designed, and often unique. They also make clean-up and maintenance easy.

The main reason that people consider Tiny Homes is sustainability/affordability. The economy world-wide is not as good as it once was, and so the Tiny Home is quite appealing. No one wants to be chained down to high mortgages, high utility bills and the stress that comes with it. With a Tiny House you have more ease of living, a smaller investment, and less work that has to be put into it once it's built.

Another reason people are going towards Tiny House living is because they are better for the environment. Modern day homes are bad for the environment for multiple reasons. Tiny Homes have large environmental benefits, and you'll leave less of an environmental footprint.

Pros & Cons of Tiny House Living

Like anything, Tiny House living isn't perfect. There are pros and cons, and tradeoffs. In this chapter, we'll explore the pros and cons of Tiny House living and what it can do for you.

The Cons:

It's important to go into this with your eyes open. If you can't reconcile yourself to the cons then maybe Tiny House living isn't for you.

1. You may not have room for a dedicated home office space – unless all you need is a phone and a computer. You might consider renting office space.

2. You may not find much no room for indoor exercise.

3. It may get hot in summer. With a Tiny House, you won't have a large roof overhang which could heat up the house and make you uncomfortable, so you'll need to turn up the AC or get ready for some heat.

4. You have to be sure that you're going to be able to handle a small kitchen, small living room, bedroom, and of course, a small bathroom.

5. With Tiny Houses, you'll have a small bathroom. This means that you have to get used to showers and no bath.

6. The dynamics of privacy and personal space may take some getting used to in Tiny House living. Without kids, this isn't usually an issue, but with kids it may take longer to adjust.

The Pros:

Now, we get to the fun part. Tiny House living does have pros that are sure to help negate the cons. It's still a lot to get used to, but these reasons are sure to help.

1. You'll have an intimate connection to the outdoors due to the ability to be close to a window at all times. You can have blinds and curtains, but you'll find that most of the time you'll want natural light – it easy to connect with nature when living in a small house.

2. Tiny Houses are much more affordable to build, and this allows you to create your own home. Often it is mortgage free which means that you won't be tied down to a huge loan. Maybe you'll be able to make some dreams come true?

3. You won't spend a lot of time cleaning because of the small space. Everything is usually easier to organize in a Tiny Home as well: you'll keep it looking tidy and efficient. Also, it is easy to communicate with others in the house to pitch in and work cooperatively.

4. You'll want to get out more. Claustrophobia is a concern, but don't want to spend all your time indoors anyway – get out and enjoy nature and your community!

5. A Tiny House is extremely cozy in winter. It's easy to warm up even when it's cold, and keeping it warm is going to be a snap as well.

6. Your bills won't be as high, and this will give you more money to spend on other things that you like. You'll find that renting the land is relatively inexpensive, and your utility bills as well. This allows you to build a better savings account for other things you want.

7. It's easy to make changes to your house. When you live in a larger house, changes are expensive, but with a Tiny House things are easier to change. You can change the color, change appliances easier since you have more money, or just rearrange whatever you want. Adding things is easy as well.

Financing a Tiny House

If you want a Tiny House, then you're going to need to finance one. The obvious way to do so is to start a savings account and wait until you have the money, but not everyone is that lucky when they're trying to save up for a home, even a Tiny Home. It's hard to estimate the cost of a Tiny House if you're doing the building yourself, and building yourself is usually the best way to do it. The cost of labor is the most expensive part of a Tiny House. You have to remember that you need to think about it as a process. The bills will come in as they come in. it won't be all at once. You need to know the cost of materials, and then you'll need to factor in labor if there is any, as well. The prices for this will vary region by region. The only thing that is certain is that the price you'll pay for building a Tiny Home is just a fraction of what you'd be paying for a real home. With most builders a Tiny Home will be very reasonable – a fraction of the prices of conventional homes. Building a Tiny Home is much more affordable.

How to Save More:

1. **Building Yourself:**

    This is the best way to save money on your Tiny Home because the labor is the costliest part. You probably already know that labor costs a lot, but you may not know that it actually costs almost double to have someone else build your house. This is why it's best to just build your house yourself. You'll need to learn a few carpentry tricks, and then doing the work yourself won't be too hard. It will be a learning experience, but it's one that will prove fruitful in the end. Doing it yourself also allows you to customize your house however you like.

2. **Creativity:**

    If you can be creative, then you're sure to save money as well. Try to learn to utilize what is readily available to you in regards to materials. You'll want to figure out how to convert logs into building materials, etc. Repurpose old, used materials as well. This will save you money.

3. **Choose Materials Carefully:**

    Unless you know what materials are available to you, you're more likely to settle for the costlier ones. You need to know what the best material is for what you're doing, and you need to know the differences between materials so that you can tell what is and isn't needed. You can still get quality materials at a cheaper price, and you won't make a mistake in building your home if you have the knowledge you need.

Financing Options:

You need to learn the financing options and then make good decisions with financing your home.

You may have to piece together one or more options to be able to build your Tiny Home.

1. **Your Own Finances:**

    It's always best to use as much of your own money as possible when building your Tiny Home. No one wants to be in debt, and this is the only way you can avoid debt. Otherwise, you'll have to worry about interest rates and getting further into debt. Sadly, not everyone has enough money in their bank account, as it takes thousands.

2. **Family & Friends:**

    Borrowing money from family and friends may hurt your pride, but it's sometimes best to borrow from someone that you're close to. Just make sure that you end up with an agreement that will benefit both of you. You don't want to take advantage of anyone so some sort of interest rate and payback agreement is in order.

    Bank Loan:

    This is one of the most common ways to get the money, and you need to remember that even if you're making payments on a loan for a Tiny House, it'll be a lot less than if you had bought a larger house. You'll have to talk to your bank about what they think is best and what is available for you based on your circumstances(sometimes people have a hard time securing a mortgage or construction loan because they are too small to qualify).

3. **Manufacturer Financing:**

   If you buy from a Tiny House manufacturer they sometimes have financing options to help you out.

   RV Loan:

   Many Tiny Houses are actually made from an RV, and if you're doing this, then you can get an RV loan. Some Tiny House manufacturers are classified as RV manufacturers, as well. You do need to know that they have a higher interest rate and you'll need a sizeable down payment. It's easier if you get approved by a credit union before you approach them asking for a loan. You will also need to factor in the additional costs, such as shipping your home.

4. **Peer-to-peer Lending:**

   Peer lending is a great way to get financed for something like a Tiny Home. The people that are investing usually want to support other people, helping them to realize their dreams. There will still be some interest charged, but you'll get a good deal.

5. **Credit Cards:**

   Credit cards are also an option when financing part of a Tiny Home, but shouldn't be relied upon exclusively as it may be very difficult to pay down the debt because of the very high interest rates.

The Houseboat

You may be thinking that all Tiny Houses are the same, but this just isn't true. There are different types of Tiny Houses, and it's important to realize this so that you can make the proper decision on what type of Tiny House you're going to try to build. It all depends on what you want and your specific needs. However, some are more favored than others. The first is the houseboat, which you'll see below.

This type of Tiny House isn't built often, as it does require you to live off of land. You'll find that there are many houseboats for sale, but you need to be able to handle disposing of your own waste, as you will not have a sewage system. You'll also need to pay docking fees, but it's great if you want to just get away from everyone and sit in the middle of nowhere for a while.

You won't be able to live in a houseboat if you're prone to motion sickness. It can cost under $2,000 a month to live on a houseboat, and many apartments will cost you more for a family. If you're designing the boat yourself and not using a mortgage, then it'll cost you even less. As far as sewage is concerned, it can cost as little as $20 to pump it out when you need to. This needs done about once a week or once every other week, depending upon the amount of people living there.

It'll cost you less if you can keep the mechanical system running yourself, but not everyone is so lucky. A normal houseboat is about three hundred square feet, and many people need to rent a storage unit. If you don't, then you'll save roughly a hundred dollars a month. When living on a houseboat, you'll need to budget for unexpected maintenance costs that may or may not come up. It's just like owning a car, and it's recommended that you save about a grand a year to make sure that you can cover anything.

There are two types of houseboats that you should be aware of. You can renovate a boat, or you can have a floating home. These are usually put on barge hulls, and you wouldn't be able to sail them to the Bahamas or some other destination that isn't in protected waters. However, either will work for Tiny House living. You've already seen a picture of a boat that has been renovated at the start of this section, but you'll see a floating house below.

There difference is mainly asthetic. It is often considered cheaper to rennovate an old boat if you learn how to make the repairs. The hardest part is rennovating a kitchen, and minimilistic is the way to go.

Some Pros & Cons:

It's important to know the pros and cons of building a house boat if you're going to think about it as the right Tiny Home for you. Let's start with the cons.

- **Con:** You'll be spending a lot of time on your own, especially when building it. It is one of the the harder Tiny Houses to build and maintain. You can still buy a hosueboat, but building one is difficult, especially due to the maintance of renovating an old boat that needs work.

- **Con:** Not every significant other is going to want to live on a boat with you. It may be a personal choice, but when you're in a realtionship, not everyone will agree. If you aren't in a relationship now, your significant other later on may not agree with it.

- **Con:** There's not much space for greenery. You won't be able to have a garden, but you will be able to have some container plants if you know how to take care of them. Growing your own food, isn't an option, and plants can be hard to sustain.

- **Pro:** You'll have large finanical savings, and you won't always need to use the grand that is reocmmended to be put back for mechanical problems. They will not always occur, and therefore you'll get into good saving habits.

- **Pro:** You'll have a base for your Tiny House, and so it's easier to get designs and start building. You'll have everything that you need already there. This usually includes the kitchen and bathroom, which are the hardest parts for most people when building a Tiny Home.

- **Pro:** You have a lower purchase price with houseboats, and you have less depreciation for it's re-sale value if you ever do have to give it up for one reason or another.

- **Pro:** If you like fishing, the hobby becomes a lot easier if you have a house boat. You can't usually grow anything, but you'll be able to catch dinner or spend hours doing something you love without having to prepare for a long trip.

About Yurts

Houseboats aren't for everyone, and so you may want to consider a yurt instead. Yurts, as seen above, are a wide open room. They are a type of affordable housing that is a simple structure that's been around for more than a thousand years. They are built with modern, contemporary materials now. It's a very solid structure that is put up very quickly, and it's considered to be quite durable.

You'll have to rent the land, but moving a yurt is rather easy, and so you'll have a variety of living options available to you. The best way to describe one is a round, portable cabin. Yurts aren't exactly costly. You can get one for around $10,000. The difference is that you need to pay for electricity to be put into it, as well as plumbing, and a water source.

This can raise the cost by $22,000 to $28,000 roughly, but prices may vary depending on where you live and if you do it yourself. You'll need a platform, as seen above, to come with your yurt to put it on. You can go for solar energy or electricity. Solar energy is going to save you money overall, but it will have a higher upfront cost. It's a choice that you have to make.

You will also have permit fees that can cost you up to $5,000. There are also land rental or land ownership fees that you'll need to think about. If you're going to move around, then you're going to just want to rent the land. If you want to stay in one place, then it's best to just buy a lot, which could cost you around another $10,000.

Pros & Cons:

Just like with any Tiny House, there are pros and cons to living in a yurt. You'll find them below.

Living in a yurt is a more popular way to live in a Tiny House.

- **Con:** Some people that live in a yurt do have problems with bugs. Yurts may be able to keep the weather out, but they aren't able to keep bugs out nearly as well.

- **Con:** Yurts have extremely small kitchens, and if you're into cooking a lot, then it is not best for you. Most yurts will not even have an oven to cook in. It's more likely you'll have a single burner.

- **Con:** A yurt will not hold heat well in the winter, and so leaving for more than a few hours will cause the yurt to become extremely cold. It does heat up fairly well, but it will take some time, and you'll most likely have to bundle up until it does. It's best to own a yurt in an area with a relatively stable climate.

- **Con:** Dishes and laundry will take longer to do because you will not have a dishwasher or washing machine. You certainly won't have a dryer, so you'll be doing all of this by hand.

- **Pro:** You do have a bathroom in a yurt. This is not necessarily true with every Tiny Home. It is hooked up to a septic system, but it's better than no bathroom at all, and it is easier to maintain. This isn't true with every yurt, but the majority of yurts do have a restroom.

- **Pro:** Yurts have a lot of natural lighting, and so you won't need to use electricity on lights until the sun goes down. This can also help with depression and stress.

- **Pro:** Making a yurt is extremely simple because it is, essentially, one large room. This means that there is not a lot of work or cost of materials. It is one of the cheaper Tiny House options, and it's easier to maintain. If you're organized, you'll feel that the room is spacious. It acts very similarly to an efficiency apartment.

- **Pro:** It is much easier to get yurts made and shipped too you, leaving it where you only have to customize it afterwards. Some companies even have customizable options. However, it is usually best that you do so yourself so that you can make your customizations more affordable.

Tiny House RV

Tiny Homes are often a type of RV as well, and these can be the easiest Tiny Homes to build. However, they are not the most popular. They are popular if you want to be able to get up and go or travel. However, you do not have as many different designs to choose from when you go with this Tiny House option. You can take an existing RV, as seen above, or you can build your own and hitch it to a vehicle, as seen below.

The second option is considered to be more stylish and customizable, but it is not the easiest to build. It takes more work, and often you'll have to build it yourself. An existing RV already has everything you need. With the RV style Tiny Home as seen above, you'll find that it had a trailer platform and was built from scratch. You'd have to buy the materials, which the one above is made of wood.

As seen above, the interior is usually much like a loft. You can have more natural lighting with various windows, but for that you need to build your own. You'll see in the picture above that there are various windows present, including a sky light to help let light in. you can get them for under $10,000, but you'll find that some are even cheaper if you aren't making them yourself. It'll cost more if you plan to customize it, as the interior above has been.

The maintenance is still less than a houseboat, but it is more maintenance than a yurt. You will need to rent land or stay at free places, which can be hard to find. Renting land will be a few hundred a month, or if you want to stay in one place you can rent a lot, which is cheaper in the long run.

However, it often defeats the purpose of choosing this type of Tiny House. One bonus is that you can get them for as little as $3,000-$5,000, depending on how much renovation you're willing to do. However, for a long time, they will not look as good as the one seen above. You can look at local listings for the best deal.

Pros & Cons:

There are less cons with RVs if you're looking for a movable lifestyle. It's not something that you just have to sit in place with, and it allows for your inner traveler to come out.

- **Con:** You have to deal with mold and mildew and be able to combat that. It's very common in small spaces, especially where moisture can collect. It's important to have something to clean mold and mildew with, and if you have asthma, this can be more of a problem than with other people.

- **Con:** RVs, as with any mobile living, make it easier for things in your home to break. You are driving on the highways and roadways at over sixty miles per hour, and this can rattle things around.

- **Con:** Small bathrooms are a con of almost any Tiny House, but it's even more prominent with RV style Tiny Houses. Just like with a houseboat, you'll have to pump out your waste as well.

- **Con:** You will have the cost of gas if you are constantly moving around, and it's important that you factor that into your budget.

- **Con:** You'll also have to repair more often than with a stable home because you're constantly experiencing wear and tear on your home due to the moving.

- **Pro:** You can camp in many spots for free, and you get to take your home with you. Everything you have is always right there. Even if it's not a lot. This allows you to live rent free, helping to negate the other costs of Tiny House living.

- **Pro:** You can move from spot to spot, and most places that you can camp for free allow you to connect with nature. This can lead to less stress and an overall sense of wellbeing.

- **Pro:** It usually only takes ten to fifteen minutes to clean up an RV style Tiny House due to the extremely small size. It is smaller than other Tiny Homes, and therefore isn't as much to take care of on a day to day basis.

- **Pro:** Due to the small size and constant movement, it's known to increase communication with those you care for, as all decisions will need to be made together.

The Traditional Tiny House

The traditional Tiny House is as pictured above. It's just a small home that is minimalistic. It has the most diversity out of them all. It allows you to customize everything as you would a normal home on a smaller scale. It allows for a variety of floorplans, roof types, gardens, and a normal plot of land. This means that you'll be able to get everything that you want from your home without having to compromise nearly as much.

Pros & Cons:

There are pros and cons with a traditional Tiny House just as there are for other times. Remember that the customization that it allows is one of the biggest pros.

- **Con:** Like any Tiny Home, you have to realize that even though this traditional option is bigger, it's still small. You will need to learn to organize and learn how to deal with claustrophobia.

- **Pro:** It's easy to renovate. You'll be able to make changes and add-ons if you need to. If you ever feel like it is too small, you can add a small room or porch. The porch is a large pro for this sort of Tiny Home.

- **Pro:** You can have a garden with this type of home, as you will have a plot of land to go with it.

- **Pro:** It has a stable, normal foundation that is less likely to need maintenance. You will also easily have electricity, cable, and running water.

Four Basic Floorplans

You already know what types of Tiny Houses you can have, but there are some basic floor plans that you'll want to look at. They can be adapted from anything to a traditional Tiny Home to one that's mobile. However, mobile homes usually do not need a floorplan, as you'll be using a preexisting structure.

Floor Plan #1

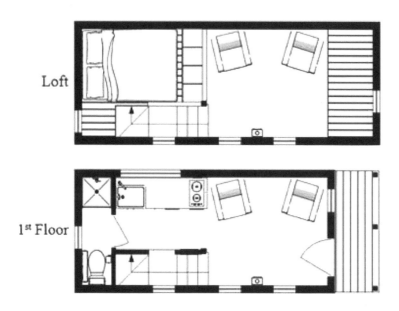

As you can see above, you'll find that most Tiny Homes are two stories unless you are getting a yurt or mobile Tiny Home. This is one of the most basic floor plans. The top floor is used for a loft, as that will be your bedroom.

The second floor is only a half-floor in this floor plan. Your bed takes up the entire area with stairs descending from it. The first floor in the bottom left, you'll find the restroom, and the kitchen is divided from it. You also have a small sitting area and then a patio that you can decorate or use as a porch. The goal of a loft is to have a small area that is just for you.

You can have a full second story, with a slight modification. This would allow for a two bedroom Tiny Home. A loft is usually not big enough for a four poster bed, and many people will have just a small frame for the boxspring and mattress to go on when they're living in a Tiny Home. One of the most popular frames is a DIY queen size bedframe made out of repurposed pallets. This is the cheapest way to build DIY furniture, which is another green way to make your Tiny Home a little more unique.

Floor Plan #2

This is another basic floor plan for a stable, traditional Tiny Home. You'll find that it has a porch, and the main room is on both sides. It's bigger, leading into the kitchen area. When the kitchen area is put at the back it is considered to be a more open floor plan. It allow for more room, but it does have just as small of a restroom as the one before.

However, you'll notice that the second floor is big enough for a queen size bed, and the loft is the entire second floor. This allows for a little more room. Though, you'll find that this floorplan is an extremely small Tiny Home, and it's only good if you are single or a couple. It does not work for children.

Floor Plan #3

This is a Tiny Home that is more for a couple that has children. It has a full two stories, and it had more than just one loft on the second story. You have a guest room, a small bathroom as well as a larger one. You also have two bedrooms, stairs, and a decently large kitchen. It also has room for a porch, and when put on a larger plot of land, you'll have more area outside where you can set an outdoor dining area or even a garden. This is a larger Tiny Home, which allows for a more detailed floor plan.

Floor Plan #4

This is also a larger Tiny Home, and it's a little more spacious as well. This design is meant to allow for more natural light to come in. the porch is a little larger, but you'll find the loft has a skylight which will allow more light in your bedroom. This will keep the home from feeling too claustrophobic. The open floor plan on the second floor gives you more space, but it does not allow for a second bedroom.

It helps people from feeling as if they're crowded or crammed into their Tiny Home. This is the best floorplan for a single person or a couple that is nervous about living in a Tiny Home. This Tiny Home has an expanded kitchen, as well as a second bedroom for either a child or a guest bedroom. It can also be turned into a home office.

A Little About Gathering Your Materials

It's challenging to build your own Tiny Home, but it can be done. The first thing you need to consider is how to gather your materials. To do this properly, you're going to need to take your time. Good things will come if you wait, but if you try to rush, you will have a harder time. You will have to compromise on various details if you want cheap, quality materials and designs.

Start with Salvage Yards:

Starting with salvage yards are a must, and if you live in a well-populated area or in a city, this should be easy. Go to scavenge for various materials. There's no reason to be worried, and it's a great way to get cheap or free lumber.

Post about It:

There are tons of people selling things on websites like Craigslist, apps like OfferUp, and even in magazines. Of course, you don't have to just scavenge for an ad. You can always just post an ad yourself, and this will allow you to find more competitive prices. They'll be offering you a good price to get the materials off their hands so that they can move on.

Don't Compromise Quality:

It's one thing to be willing to compromise, but be careful. The first thing you should never compromise on is the standard of material. It's sometimes hard to turn down a good offer, and you may even find free offers for materials. However, don't take anything that you don't want to use in your home. Just keep in mind that it is your home, and you'll be living in it. It should be sturdy. Compromise on what materials you use, but not on the quality of that material.

How to Salvage Materials:

You may like the idea of salvaged materials, but that doesn't mean you know how to go about finding them. You can check people's driveways for throwaways where they've bought too much. You can also talk to people who are just finishing a renovation if you see them, and offer to buy the left over materials for cheap so that they get some return on them, and they'll be kept in better condition than just being thrown in the driveway. You can also ask your friends and family if they know anyone or have anything that they're no longer going to use. This will allow you to build in an environmentally friendly way that won't break your bank.

Buying From the Store:

Sadly, salvaged materials are not always an option, and you'll have to buy at least a little from the store. So you'll find that there are benefits from buying your supplies from the store. You know that they're in good condition, and you can often even find reviews that will tell you how good the quality of that material is. You'll also have people to ask if you're unsure what material would be best for what you're looking for. Just remember that they are there to sell you a product, and so make sure that you don't feel pressured when buying.

The Tools You Need:

If you are determined, you're going to succeed. You'll need to be creative and determined, but you'll also need to be able to know you have the tools necessary. That's what this section is all about. You'll avoid countless frustrations by having the right tools on hand in the first place.

- **Drill & Impact Driver:** This tool is a must, and you'll be using it for a variety of tasks when building your Tiny Home. It'll be useful when framing with screws, but you'll need a well-built drilling machine. This will most likely be heavy and solid feeling.

- **Tape Measure:** It may seem like common sense, but having a tape measure on hand will save you countless time and frustration. It's necessary for accuracy, and if you don't use it, then everything will start to go wrong.

- **Drill Bit Set:** This is required for drills so that you'll have every kind of drill you need. Of course, you'll need an accessory set as well, which include a screwdriver as well as bit adapters. It'll help you to tackle various sized holes without any setbacks. Look for having flat, hex, and sockets.

- **Tool Belt:** Again, this may seem like it is common sense, but not always. You can't hold everything you need at once, and so you'll need a tool belt to make sure that you have everything on hand. This will save you time, and you'll use it to hold onto hammers, tapes, screws, nails and so much more. It's best to have a leather belt that's heavy duty.

- **Carpenter Pencils:** This is a tool that's easy to forget, but it's essential for framing as well as sheathing. It's needed for various measurements, and it'll make sure that you make a lot less mistakes.

- **Speed Square:** When you're framing a Tiny House this isn't a must, but it's really useful. It'll help you to check for perfection, making perfect corners.

- **Leatherwork Gloves:** This will save your hands, and it's good for safety. Without them, you may get blisters, especially if you aren't used to hard work. It'll also keep your hands from getting stained up.

- **Caulking Gun:** This will help to make sure that you don't have leaks in your house. You'll need to caulk with an adhesive, and the best way to do so properly is with the use of this tool.

- **Hammer:** Hammers drive in nails, as you're sure to already know. You'll need plenty of nails, and different types at that. You'll want a hammer that will last because you will need repairs from time to time on your home. Tiny Homes have less maintenance than larger homes, but they don't maintain themselves.

- **Safety Goggles:** This is for safety reasons, but it's a must or you may get flying debris in your eyes.

For Lighting & Conditioning

Tiny Homes still need lighting and air conditioning. They can get surprisingly hot during the summer. You'll need to know what materials you need as well. You'll need to power the house. There's no reason to be unprepared.

AC Requirements:

The first thing you need to remember is that an air conditioner should be small, and it's best if it's portable. If your house is on wheels, this is even more important. However, a non-portable one will be okay if you have a stable, traditional Tiny Home.

- You'll also want your air conditioner to be affordable, and you shouldn't have to spend more than about $300. You can look around and compare prices and features. Get one that will fit your requirements. If it has a 24-hour timer feature, then you'll already be at an advantage.

- Look for a compact design so that you won't have anything that's too bulky or hard to install. Make sure that it also has a self-evaporative system so that you avoid mold and mildew.

- If you're building a Tiny Home, you're more than likely going to be living off grid. This means you'll be using wind or solar power, so you'll need to make sure that you're getting an energy saving model.

- You'll also want a dehumidifier which is environmentally friendly to make sure that you're living in the proper environment.

A Little about Lighting:

Lighting a Tiny Home is considered to be a little easier than lighting a regular sized home. You have less rooms to start with, and so you need to make sure that your energy is still in proportion to the available power, especially if you're using solar or wind. Remember that heating and cooking is not easy to sustain on these sources of power, and so your lighting should be as natural as possible.

This is why Tiny Homes usually have more windows. You won't have different lighting effects anymore, and therefore you won't have as high of energy usage. It's rare that you'll need artificial lighting, so it's important to put energy saving bulbs, solar bulbs, and battery powered bulbs in your Tiny Home. Solar powered bulbs are sure to help you light your home naturally. Wind power is best used for lighting during winters.

Building Your Kitchen

No matter what home you're going to be in, you'll need a kitchen. Everyone needs to eat, and you can't always rely on fast food. However, your kitchen can't occupy too much of your home, but it still should be able to fit all of your personal needs as well as your cooking habits.

Some Steps for Building:

You may still be able to get your dream kitchen, but it'll require you to be able to compromise. Following these building steps below, it'll help you to make sure that you have a kitchen that is small, efficient and you can be proud of.

1. **Cooking Power:** You'll first need to think about your cooking power. If you're going off-grid, it's best to choose solar power. Wind power just won't be enough. However, natural gas will usually work as well. Liquid propane is a great way to cook, and you'll be able to conserve energy with it as well.

2. **Think about Numbers:** You need to think about the number of people you're going to be cooking for when you're building your kitchen. You'll need a larger kitchen if you have a larger number of people. It'll require more daily food consumption, which will require more storage space as well as cooking supplies.

3. **Think Requirements:** It's also important that you think about all of the requirements that you use when cooking. Think about what you need, and then think about your luxuries when cooking. Try to eliminate as many luxuries as you can, and you'll soon learn to cook without them, which will help you to downsize so that you can fit everything into a smaller kitchen.

4. **Think Budget:** You can't just ignore your budget. Even when building your dream home. Even a Tiny Home can get expensive, and your budget will determine how big of a kitchen you'll be able to build. If you're on a tighter budget, you'll need to strip away more luxuries so that you can make sure that you have a kitchen that is functional. It being functional is the most important part, and you may need to go with the bare essentials.

5. **Set Space:** You'll need to set up space as well for a refrigerator, but you shouldn't need a large one unless you have a large family. With a Tiny Home, you may have to go shopping more often because you won't have that much room, especially if you choose to eat a raw diet.

Some Kitchen Options:

It's important to have a conservative option for a Tiny House, and there's a few more things you'll need to think about.

Layout: Layout is extremely important, and you need to choose one that ensures that your kitchen is efficient. It's important to be creative, but you do need to think about what will be best for you. Make sure that everything is within range to grab easily, and that means you'll want your sink, cooking range, and fridge within arm's reach so that you'll be able to keep everything clean.

Countertops: An economical kitchen will be important, but you'll also need some space for countertops. You won't be able to cook without them. This is where you'll be preparing your meal. What type of countertops you get will depend on your budget and design plans.

Ovens & Ranges: Not everyone actually needs and oven, so ask yourself if you really do. If you have the room, need, or even just the money you may want to add at least a small oven. However, always keep in mind that an oven will actually consume a lot of energy, which can be hard if you're living off the grid. It's not sustainable in most Tiny Homes.

Refrigerator: Going off the grid, doesn't mean that you have to get rid of the refrigerator. It does mean that you'll want a propane or solar powered one.

Putting in a Restroom

You don't want to skip out on a restroom, even if you're building a Tiny Home. However, you'll need to keep in mind that your space is still limited. In some cases, it is extremely limited. When you use the space properly, you'll be able to put in a restroom. There are many different types of toilets that you'll need to consider though.

You'll first want to keep in mind about cost so that you get something that is affordable as well as suitable for your needs. Make sure that you stay within your budget. You'll also want to do your research first so that you know that you're buying the right one. Get something that separates solid waste from urine if possible, as it'll help to reduce odor, especially if you don't have normal plumbing. There are a few things that you need to consider.

RV Low Flush Toilets:

These are great for almost any Tiny Home, but they're especially great if you're using a Tiny Home that's mobile. However, you'll need to empty them regularly, as discussed before. This will be a weekly charge. You can still use this type of toilet if you're connected to a sewage system as well, which will have it drained directly. It's a very small facility, but it doesn't harbor bad smells, and it's also very clean. You need to have fresh water for this to be an option.

An Incinerating Toilet:

This is a toilet that you're going to want to consider if there isn't a lot of water. This connects to power, however. You'll need a power source, but it'll burn all of your waste to ash, and then you'll just need to empty the ash. You can do this about once a week or when you deem fit. It all depends on you. Though, they can be quite expensive, and it'll use a lot of power on top of it.

Composting Toilets:

This is another option for your toilet, especially if you want to be environmentally friendly. You'll need aeration and ventilation as well. It'll take your solid waste to decompose, but it will allow urine to be diverted into a small holding system that will need dumped out. They are self-contained, and they can be done with or without water. It's even able to be used with or without power. It's great if you're short on space, and these toilets can even be put outside.

Showers:

Showers are a must as well. Even in your Tiny Home, but you need to keep in mind that you most likely won't have room for a tub. You can get a shower that is already built in, or you can get one that can be attached inside or outside of your home if your Tiny Home is stable. If you're trying to keep your shower room separate, you'll want to have a tie back onto the wall, which will allow you to feel as if you have bigger space. It's an illusion, but it can help to avoid claustrophobia.

A fiberglass shower is also a great idea, and it gives you an open shower plan which will allow you to contain the splashing of water. It'll be a shower enclosure, which can help you to save on space. You can always look for ideas in home magazines, and you'll even find many designs on the web. Look for what's efficient, trending, and what doesn't require a lot of energy or upkeep.

Tiny Home Tips

There are a few tips that you may need to make sure that living in Tiny House is comfortable for you. It'll help you to adjust to this new style of living and feel comfortable right away.

Tip #1 Window to Wall Ratio

It's important to look at your window to wall ration when you're trying to move to a smaller space. By having larger windows, your space won't seem nearly as small, and it'll help you to make sure that you feel comfortable. Use as many windows as possible, and having one on every wall is usually a good option. Don't forget about skylights as well, which will allow for more natural light to come into the room. This will also make sure that you don't fall into anxiety, stress or even depression.

Tip #2 Bookshelves & More Bookshelves

It's important to install shelves or bookshelves in your Tiny House. This will give you more storage area, and floor to ceiling bookshelves are recommended so that you can get the most out of your space. It'll help to make sure that you don't forget anything, and you'll be able to have everything at arm's reach. It's even better if you have a lot of books or nick knacks that you don't want to get rid of when moving to your Tiny Home. It may even mean that you won't need to get a storage unit after weeding out the junk.

Tip #3 Semi-Opaque Materials

It's important to use semi-opaque materials when building a windowless room, as it'll allow more light to come in. remember that one wall can double as two. You can separate your kitchen from your bathroom with an opaque wall to make sure that your bathroom isn't dark without the need for light most of the time.

Tip #4 Utilize the Outdoors

You're going to want to create an outdoor living space if you want to make it seem like you have more space than you do. Patios and gardens are a great way to do this. You won't need to add square footage, and it'll get you outside more often. Even adding a porch won't add too much to your budget, which will help you to feel like you aren't as restricted when moving to such a smaller living area.

Tip #5 Add Lofts When You Can

You can use lofts for more than just your bedroom. Add a loft wherever you can. Even when you can't have a second bedroom. It'll help to make sure that you have spaces that people can go to so that you can get away from everything. It'll also help with storage areas, or you can give yourself a dedicated work area with a loft if you don't need a lot.

Tip #6 Use less Walls

You're going to want to use less walls as well. This may seem silly at first, but having a multipurpose room will make your house seem that much bigger. Do you really need to put a wall between the living room and the kitchen? No, not really. This will make it seem larger, and so each room won't seem crowded.

Tip #7 Go Under the Stairs

You don't want to leave the space under the stairs empty. You don't want to leave any space empty. These are places that you can organize materials. It'll help you to utilize every ounce of space you have, and under the stairs you can put shelves, boxes, or something that rolls out so that you can get to it. You can even put a chair if you don't feel that you're squeezing too much into it. Add shelves wherever something else doesn't fit.

Tip #8 Sliding Walls

You don't always need a door. Sometimes you do want to close things off. If you do want a wall between your kitchen and your living room, try a sliding wall. This means that you'll be able to change your design whenever you want to. It won't feel nearly as confining. However, when you need a little more peace and privacy, especially if you live with others, sliding walls can double as a way to escape the crowded living quarters.

Tip #9 Room Dividers

Room dividers are way to open your space as well. It'll even help to make sure that you don't have to feel as if things are closed off. It'll allow more light as well. You can use glass walls for the same reason. Though, glass walls are not recommended if you have children, as it can be dangerous.

Tip #10 Use Decorative Lights

Decorating is important in your Tiny Home, and decorating with lights is a must. It'll help to make sure that everything is unique, well lit, and it'll help to make sure that you are making your space look a little wider. A dark space will always seem a little smaller.

Tip #11 Lower Furniture

You don't want furniture to be too tall, or it won't look like you have any vertical space. It'll look like your house is more crowded, so low sitting furniture is a must. Be careful when you're looking for furniture. You don't want anything that is too big. Make sure that you grab your tape measure so that everything fits perfectly.

Tip #12 Add Color

This may seem obvious, but you need to add color to your Tiny Home. Color helps to widen the space, and it helps to make sure that you don't fall into depression. Changing from a normal house to a smaller house is a hard change. Stave off depression as much as you can.

Tip #13 Retractable Drawers

This is especially important in the kitchen, but retractable drawers will allow you to take up less space and still hold the same amount. It'll also help you to seem like it's less cluttered even if it does take up the same amount of space in some instances. Clutter will make you feel like your house is smaller than it actually is.

Buying Vs. Building

There are pros and cons to buying a Tiny Home versus building a Tiny Home. If you build your home, you'll be able to be satisfied completely with your home. However, it can be a little overwhelming as well. Though, you'll need to remember that it is not easy to build and customize your home. It's an ongoing process, and it'll take you time to get everything right.

This can cause a high level of frustration, and you may not be satisfied because of your limited experiences. However, all customizations will be an ongoing process for your house. It doesn't matter if you're buying or building, as you'll eventually need to put some of your own work into it. It all depends on how much work you're willing to do and how much time you're willing to spend.

Buying a Tiny Home:

- **Pro:** You don't have to put in as much work, so you won't have to suffer the frustration of building your own house. This is especially important if you don't have a lot of skill with carpentry.

- **Pro:** You don't have to worry about not getting the proper materials to build your home. You have an expert telling you what will be a sustainable home.

- **Pro:** You'll get your Tiny Home in a lot less time. Building your own home is time consuming. It can take six months to a year or even longer.

- **Con:** You will have to deal with something that is pre-designed. This means that you won't get your dream house most likely unless you have a high budget and are able to order something custom.

- **Con:** You'll need almost all of the money up front. You can get a loan, but it's much harder since it's a Tiny Home and less options will be available.

- **Con:** You'll be spending more on your house because you'll also be paying the cost of labor as well. This can double the price, but it does ensure quality. You can shop around for who you want to build your house. However, no matter who you get, a professional will be expensive.

Building a Tiny Home:

There are pros and cons to consider with taking on the task of building your Tiny Home as well. Just remember that you need to be able to handle the process, and if you aren't good with your hands, it's not going to be nearly as easy.

- Pro: You'll be able to make everything custom. There's nothing that you won't be able to add if you want to unless you feel that you're incapable.

- Pro: You won't have to deal with finding a contractor and entering into a contract. There will be no legal issues besides permits.

- Pro: Every material is chosen by you so that you know exactly what you'll be getting. You shouldn't be disappointed about anything or find out about anything later on after the fact.

- Con: Fatigue and stress will be an issue. It's not easy to build something, and it's not easy to build something so large, either.

- Cons: You have to figure out every type of permit you need by yourself or hire someone to help you with either way. You'll also need to figure out insurance all by yourself.

- Con: It's harder to build a mobile home that won't tear apart. It's going to limit the types of Tiny Homes that you can build properly.

Conclusion

Now you know how to live in your Tiny Home. From knowing if you should build or buy your Tiny Home to how to decorate it to make it feel less restricting, you have all the knowledge you need to get started. You can take that next step into minimalistic living, helping you to get everything in order.

Just remember that with these tips and tricks, it's easier, but it's still an adjustment. You can't expect to adjust to the change overnight. If you're building your Tiny House, you'll get used to the idea a lot slower, helping you to adjust a little easier.

www.ingramcontent.com/pod-product-compliance
Lightning Source LLC
LaVergne TN
LVHW070428110925
820836LV00001B/2